Oh, No! Why Me? II

By
Robin
Wasserman

SCHOLASTIC INC.

New York   Toronto   London   Auckland   Sydney
Mexico City   New Delhi   Hong Kong   Buenos Aires

*For Susie and Jessica, who are always
laughing with me, not at me.
I think.*

ISBN 0-439-45293-7

12 11 10 9 8 7 6 5 4 3 2 1   2 3 4 5 6 7/0

Printed in the U.S.A.   40
First printing, October 2002

Contents

WHY ME?

You know the feeling. They're all looking at you. Everybody. And they're all laughing. Their eyes are burning into your skin, and you can feel your face heating up and turning that attractive lobster red. You've just done something totally, completely humiliating, and you are never, ever going to show your face in public again!

Or, at least, that's how it feels. But before you grab several years' supply of junk food and hide out in your room until it's time for college, there are a couple of things you should know:

1. **It happens to everyone.**
2. **You will get through it.**

Okay, you may not believe it now, but it's true. Everyone has their totally embarrassing moments — your teachers, your parents, your favorite rock stars, and all those Hollywood hotties, not to mention every single person you know at school. That's right — your BFFs, your crushes, even the coolest kids, the ones who always seem to have it all together. So don't waste your time asking, "Why me?" The world isn't out to get you — even though it may seem that way sometimes! Everyone has their miserable moments, and everyone gets through them.

Want proof? Turn the page — you'll find page after page of embarrassing stories from kids just like you. Whatever embarrassment you've been through, chances are, you'll find someone in here who's had it even worse.

And guess what — they all made it out alive!

FOOL IN SCHOOL

Let's face it. School is tough enough — you've got homework, tests, friends, and boys to deal with, not to mention strict teachers, not-so-interesting classes, and that mysterious cafeteria food. The last thing you need is something else to deal with — especially if it's something like making a fool of yourself in front of everyone you know! But since you spend most of your time in school, chances are, you're probably going to do something embarrassing there at least once before you graduate. Hey, at least you're not alone!

Trapped!

I was at the high school for our district spelling bee, and some friends and I decided to go exploring. We eventually found a door that opened out into a courtyard. It was a warm, sunny day, so we went outside — but when we tried to get back in, the door into the school was locked! The whole courtyard was surrounded by a fence. We were trapped! But that's not the most embarrassing part. My friends decided we should just climb over the fence to get out — and so they did. Then I tried. But I'm such a total klutz that I couldn't make it over. I had to wait in the courtyard by myself while my friends went to find someone to open the door. They came back with a super cute high school guy, who let me back into the building. He couldn't understand why I hadn't just climbed over the fence. So my not-so-loyal friends explained that every time I had tried to pull myself over the fence, I had just fallen down. He seemed to think that was the funniest thing he'd ever heard, and my friends just laughed along. I didn't speak to them for a week!

Ashley***

***Some names have been changed to protect the innocent — and the totally humiliated!

Better Late Than Never

It was the first day of junior high, and I was *so* ready. I'd picked out my outfit days before, and I was all set to go a whole hour before I had to leave. The school is near my house, so I was planning to walk. My mom offered to drive me, since it was the first day and I'd never been there before. But I wanted to be on my own, so I insisted on walking. Well, the school is ten minutes away, but an hour after I left my house, I was still walking. Even though the school is practically in my own neighborhood, I had gotten totally lost! I didn't know what to do. I didn't know where I was, and I was so hot and tired from walking around for so long. I just sat down on the curb and started crying. Finally, one of my mom's friends drove by and saw me there. She took me to school. So that's how I started junior high: an hour late, all hot and sweaty, and eyes totally red from crying. It was *not* a great way to start the year.

Alexis

HOW TO FACE THE MORNING AFTER

So yesterday morning something incredibly embarrassing happened to you, and you spent the whole day desperately waiting for the bell to ring. And finally, it did! You ran home in tears, raced to your bedroom, shut the door, and breathed a sigh of relief. Alone at last! Problem solved, right?

Not exactly.

Because sooner or later — and it always seems like sooner — morning comes, and you have to head out the door, down the stairs, and . . . back to school. Unless you plan to play sick for the rest of your life, you don't have much of a choice. How do you handle the dreaded moment?

With total cool. Remember, yesterday was a long time ago. Maybe you've been thinking 24/7 about what happened to you, but everyone else has probably been thinking about boys, homework, or what they're going to have for lunch. So there's no need to shake and shiver at the thought of facing everyone. Tomorrow is a brand-new day.

Even if you don't believe this, even if you can't put the past behind you so quickly (and if you can't, you're certainly not the only one), just pretend you can. *Acting* calm is the first step to *being* calm. As a bonus, if you act like yesterday never happened, hopefully everyone else will, too.

So, even if your stomach is clenching with nerves, just smile, hold your head up high, and hope for the best! You may think you'll never be able to feel comfortable at school again, but you will — and probably sooner than you think.

Help! I've Fallen and I Can't Get Up!

It was our annual awards ceremony, and I was getting a science award. My parents and my grandparents were all there to watch me. They were all so proud of me. The principal called my name, and I walked up onstage to get the award. But just as I got to him, I tripped over my own feet — and I didn't just fall down, I knocked him down, too! The whole audience started cheering and applauding. I grabbed the award and ran down the stairs and back to my seat as fast as I could. For days afterward, every time someone saw me in the hall, they'd back up and say, "Watch out, here comes Janie!"

Janie

Blowing in the Wind

I was giving the graduation speech at my middle school graduation, and my entire family was there to see me. The parents and other audience members were all sitting in front of me, and my whole class was sitting behind me. Everything was going fine until I felt a sudden gust of wind. I heard a couple of giggles behind me, and then the whole class burst into laughter. The wind had blown my skirt up! I didn't know what to do, so I just kept going on with the speech — but the wind kept blowing and my skirt kept flying! The parents out in front didn't realize what was going on, but the class couldn't stop laughing. The next thing I knew, the vice principal had rushed up behind me. She spent the rest of my speech on her knees, holding onto the back of my skirt. I've never talked so fast in my life — I couldn't wait to get through that speech and sit down!

Patricia

Food for Thought

One day at lunchtime, I had just loaded my tray up with food and was walking back to my table, when I tripped and dropped the tray. All of the food fell off, my plate cracked, and food and chocolate milk spattered everywhere — all over the floor and all over me. Then I heard it: "Oooooh . . ." Everyone in the room was looking at me and laughing. I hurried back to my table and spent the rest of lunchtime with my head down. I didn't even have anything to eat — I'd spent all my lunch money on the food that was now being mopped off the floor.

Lola

Three Cheers

At the end of the year, my school has something called Spirit Week. Each day has a different theme. On one day you're supposed to wear green and white (our school colors), on another day you're supposed to wear a hat, and so on. Monday was pajama day, so I found my old Bugs Bunny pajamas, put them on, and went to school. I thought I looked pretty cute. But as soon as I got to school I knew something was terribly wrong — no one else was wearing pajamas! It turned out that Spirit Week wasn't starting until the next Monday. I had to spend the whole day in my pajamas, while everyone laughed and called me "Bugs."

Samantha

Look Out Below!

I get carsick and seasick all the time, so when I heard my class was going on a boat cruise, I wasn't quite as excited as everyone else. But I figured that I would make the best of things — if I forced myself not to get sick, then I just wouldn't. So I put on my cutest top and mini-skirt and set off for the boat. And I looked pretty good. But as soon as the boat set sail, I realized that this was never going to work. After only a few minutes, I was already leaning over the side, trying not to be sick. Well, the good news is that I didn't throw up. The bad news is that I got so dizzy that I fell over the railing and into the water! One of the crew had to jump in and rescue me. That was the end of the boat cruise. Needless to say, I was the only one happy about that!

Kiwa

Free at Last

We were studying fruit flies in science, and each of us had a test tube filled with the tiny bugs. I always thought it was kind of sad that the bugs were trapped in the little tubes. I knew they would rather be flying free. I tried explaining this to my BFF, and as I was talking to her, I accidentally knocked half the test tubes onto the floor! They cracked, and a swarm of fruit flies escaped into our classroom. They were everywhere! We had to have class in the art room for the rest of the week while the exterminator cleaned everything out. At least the flies had a taste of freedom!

Hallie

You May Want to Sit Down for This One

I still get embarrassed just thinking about this. One day I was sitting down to lunch, and just as I sat down in my chair, it broke. And when I say it broke, I mean it cracked, loudly. Then it crashed to the floor — and I crashed down with it. The entire cafeteria saw what happened and just started laughing at me. It was so horrible and humiliating — and it didn't help when some people started calling me "The Elephant" and asking me what else I'd broken lately!

Sarah

Have a Nice Trip?

Last semester, my class built a model medieval castle out of sugar cubes. It took us weeks and weeks, but it was worth it. Our principal liked it so much that he wanted to display it in the lobby for parent-teacher night. So all we had to do was get it to the lobby. Our teacher picked a few people, including me, to help carry it downstairs. I felt pretty important that I got to help, and I was super careful. But apparently, not careful enough. Halfway down the stairs, I tripped. I threw out my hands to try to catch my fall — which means I let go of the model. I didn't fall, but the model did! It broke in half. Three weeks of work totally down the drain! My class was mad at me for weeks.

Chavonne

And the Band Played On

I play the clarinet in the school marching band. At one game, after we finished our halftime concert, I stayed on the field to talk to some of my friends. Before I realized it, the football team was running back onto the field, right toward us! My friends all got out of the way, but I didn't realize what was going on until it was too late. The players ran right by me and accidentally knocked me down in the mud — in front of everyone! The worst thing of all was that the next day the principal ordered the entire football team to write a letter of apology to me. For the rest of the season, every time one of the football players saw me in the hall, they cried, "Watch out, it's the band girl!" and ran in the other direction.

Lia

Not Quite the Iron Chef

Whenever we have a school party, everyone in class has to bring in a snack. This year, for our winter party, I decided that I was going to bake a cake all by myself. I followed the recipe really carefully and made a beautiful and very chocolaty cake. Everyone was so impressed when I brought it in the next day — they couldn't wait to eat it, and I couldn't wait to hear how much they liked it! My teacher cut the cake and handed a piece to everyone. Then the first person took a bite and spit it right back out again. Suddenly, all over the classroom, people were spitting out the cake and complaining. "This is the worst cake I've ever tasted," the boy next to me said. I took a bite, and that's when it hit me. Instead of putting in a cup of sugar, I must have put in a cup of *salt*! It was the worst cake I'd ever tasted, too. Fortunately, we had plenty of other food to eat. But trust me, the next time I baked something, I asked my parents for help!

Katie

Me and My Big Mouth

Whenever my teacher, Mrs. Donovan, leaves the classroom for some reason, she tells us to be quiet until she gets back. Of course we don't listen — in fact, after a few minutes, it usually gets so loud in there that you have to yell just to make yourself heard. One day, Mrs. Donovan smelled really bad. As soon as she left the room, we all started talking about it. The classroom was so loud that I had to yell to my friend, "Mrs. Donovan smells like sweaty old gym socks!" Just as I said it, the room went totally silent. My loud voice was the only thing you could hear. I turned around and saw that everyone had stopped talking because Mrs. Donovan was standing in the doorway. I wanted to crawl under my desk and stay there for the rest of the year.

Margaret

Sweet Dreams

My math class is really boring, so sometimes, no matter how hard I try to stay awake, I fall asleep. I can't help it. Fortunately, I sit in the back of the classroom, so my teacher usually doesn't notice. But one day, when I was really tired, I put my head down on my arms and closed my eyes. Just for a minute, I told myself. But of course, I fell asleep. When I woke up, the room was totally empty — except for my teacher, who was sitting at the front of the room, waiting for me to wake up. I'd slept through the whole class, even the bell! Instead of yelling at me, my teacher sent me home with a note, suggesting that I see a doctor. She just couldn't believe that anyone would fall asleep in her class — she thought there must have been something wrong with me!

Maureen

BOY BLUNDERS

Think about it: If having a crush were fun, they wouldn't call it a "crush." And there's nothing more crushing than doing something stupid in front of the boy you like. Why is it that every time something embarrassing happens to make you look like an idiot, there's a cute boy watching? Hey, look on the bright side: Let's say you do accidentally spit on him, knock him down, or throw up on him — if he sticks around, chances are, it's true love.

Brace Face

I was at the mall with my friend, and we stopped to get something to eat in the food court. Afterward, we decided to do some more shopping and headed over to our favorite record store. I couldn't believe it — there was Jared, a cutie from my English class, looking in the window. I went over to talk to him and was so excited the whole time that I couldn't stop smiling. And since he kept staring at my mouth, I figured I must have a pretty great smile. After he left, I ran over to my friend to give her the full 411 on the convo. But as soon as I opened my mouth, she said, "Ew, gross, you have the hugest piece of spinach caught in your braces." She couldn't have mentioned it sooner?

Barbara

My Lips Are Sealed (or Should Have Been)

Every year, the sixth graders in my school take a class trip to the local amusement park. I was having the best day, because Jamal, the boy I was crushing on, was going on all the rides with us. At the end of the day, everyone wanted to go on the one ride we'd missed: Hercules. It was the biggest coaster in the park, and even though I'm totally scared of roller coasters, I agreed to go. Jamal said he wanted to sit next to me! How could I resist? The ride was just as horrible as I'd expected it to be, and once it was over, I felt so sick and dizzy. When we got off, Jamal turned to me and said, "Well, that wasn't so bad, was it?" When I opened my mouth to answer, I couldn't help myself — I threw up all over him! *I* was totally grossed out, so I can only imagine what he must have been thinking!

Susie

E-mail Emergency

One night, my crush sent me an e-mail asking about that day's homework. I was so excited to hear from him, I forwarded it right to my BFF, saying, "Can you believe he e-mailed me? I wonder if it means he likes me b/c I LOVE him." I sent the message — and then shrieked. Instead of hitting *forward*, I had hit *reply*! I sent the message back to my crush! I tried everything I could think of, but I couldn't get the e-mail back again! I quickly e-mailed my crush to tell him that the e-mail had just been a joke, but I know he didn't believe me. Now I check and double-check every e-mail before I send it — I'm never making *that* mistake again!

Bree

Sweet Tooth

My parents don't let me eat candy unless it's a special occasion. But I love chocolate, so sometimes I buy a candy bar from the vending machine at school and eat it on my walk home. I figure they'll never know! Well, one day, just as I was about to take a bite out of my illegal candy bar, I dropped the whole thing in the dirt. I couldn't believe it! Since no one was around, I decided to go for it. I picked up the candy bar, brushed it off, and then took a bite out of it as if nothing had happened. That's when I realized there *was* someone around — the hottie who lives next door to me. He was walking home, too, and he saw the whole thing. "What, do your parents not feed you or something?" he asked. Then he laughed and walked off. I'd always wished that he would notice me — but not like that!

Aparna

Caught in the Act

All the girls in our class love Dave R. He's so handsome, he looks like a movie star. Which is why, one day in class, I wrote a note to my friend that said: *Doesn't Dave R. look handsome in his new haircut? What a hottie!* I dropped it on the ground and kicked it over to my best friend, just like always. And even though my teacher is usually so oblivious that she wouldn't notice if an elephant dropped on our classroom, she noticed this. She called me up to the front of the room and made me read my note out loud to the whole class. They all burst into laughter, and I desperately wished a big hole would open up in the floor, and I could just fall into it and disappear. No such luck.

Jamie

HOW TO SPOT HIS HUMILIATION

You may not believe it, but boys get embarrassed, too. Sure, they can be loud and gross and act like they don't care what people think of them. But guess what: They do, just as much as you! Check out these totally mortifying moments.

A Fond Farewell

My dad usually drives me to school, but one day, he had to go into work early, so my great-aunt took me instead. I was embarrassed enough when she pulled up to our house wearing her flowered housecoat and pink curlers in her hair. But I crossed my fingers and hoped that no one at school would see me get out of the car. Fat chance. Instead, my great-aunt insisted on walking me into the classroom and then planting kisses all over my face while the whole class was watching. When she finally let go and turned to leave, I thought my nightmare was over. But on the way out of the classroom, she turned back to wave and then used the nickname she's always had for me: "Have a good day at school, Mushy Tushie!" I thought I would never live it down!

Alex

HOW TO SPOT HIS HUMILIATION

Pimple Problems

I usually don't get a lot of zits, but when I do get one, it's a BIG one. The night before the school dance, I got my biggest zit ever. When I looked in the mirror, it was all I could see! I made my dad take me to the store to buy some fancy cream that promised "instant acne relief." I rubbed it on the zit, crossed my fingers, and went to sleep. The next morning, I looked in the mirror. Well, no one was going to notice the zit anymore, but only because the whole area around my zit had turned a dark purple, thanks to that stupid cream! I wanted to spend the whole night hiding in my bedroom, but my friends convinced me to go. It was just as bad as I'd expected. Toward the end of the night, the deejay announced that the next song was dedicated to "Grape Face," then played "I Heard It Through the Grapevine." Everyone in the auditorium turned to look at me and laugh. By the end of the night my face wasn't purple anymore — it was bright red!

Mark

Look, No Hands!

One afternoon, I was riding my bike around the house of this girl I sort of like. I noticed that she was lying out on her lawn reading, so I decided to show off a little for her. I took both hands off the handlebars and waved at her. I was going smoothly at first, but just as I passed by her, I lost my balance. I lost control of the bike, rammed into the curb, and flew over the handlebars. I don't think she was too impressed. Fortunately, I didn't break anything — except my bike. When my parents heard how I broke it, they promised me that I wouldn't be getting another one for a long, long time.

Tom

Look Behind You . . .

My BFF and I were standing by our lockers talking about Jordan, the cutest boy in school. I was going on and on about how cute he was — how much I loved his silky hair and his cool clothes and his beautiful eyes. My best friend kept trying to stop me. I figured it was just because she was bored — I talk about Jordan *a lot*. So I just kept going, wondering whether he liked me as much as I liked him. Then I said, "I wonder if he even knows my name." That's when someone tapped me on the shoulder. I turned around and — OMG — it was Jordan. He smiled, said, "Hi, *Grace*," then walked away. I wanted to climb into my locker and stay there for the rest of the school year!

Grace

Busted!

I was having a sleepover, and we were playing truth or dare. I picked dare, and someone dared me to call my crush, Robbie Jackson, and then hang up. I was so nervous, but a dare's a dare — I did it. As soon as he answered, I slammed down the phone, and we all burst into giggles. A few minutes later, my phone rang, and I picked it up without thinking. I heard a man's voice say, "This is Mike Jackson — did someone here call me?" It was Robbie's father! He'd star 69'd me. I didn't know what to do. I whispered, "Sorry, wrong number," and slammed the phone down again. It took an hour for all my friends to stop laughing at me!

Mimi

Sorry, Wrong Number

I had a huge crush on one of my best guy friends, but I was afraid he didn't feel the same way. I moaned about my problem to everyone I knew. One day, as I was spilling my guts to my BFF about the latest super cute thing that Jim had done, I realized that I'd bumped my cell phone and accidentally redialed the last number I called. My heart almost stopped as I tried to figure out who it was. But deep down, I already knew — it was Jim. And I was right — he'd heard the whole conversation!

Anica

A Crushing Blow

One day, I heard the best rumor of my life: A cute boy in another class had a big crush on me, but he was too shy to find out whether I liked him, too. Of course I did — he was the cutest boy in school! At lunch, I wrote him a mushy love letter, telling him how cute I thought he was and that I totally liked him. Then, since I was too shy to give it to him, I just stuck it in his locker. Later in the day, I found out that it was all a big joke — he didn't have a crush on me. He didn't even know who I was. Well, he does now!

Amalia

Here He Comes . . . and There He Goes

Josh is so hot. Have you seen Tom Cruise? Brad Pitt? Compared to Josh, they're nothing. Which is why I was so excited when I saw him waving at me from across the hall. I didn't think Josh even knew who I was! So I smiled and waved at him, and he grinned back. Then he actually started walking over to me! I didn't know what to do — I patted my hair down to make sure it looked okay and made my best friend tell me if I had anything in my teeth. He got closer and closer . . . and then he walked right past me. I turned around, only to see him throw his arm around the tall blond girl standing behind me. He'd been looking at her the whole time. I felt like such an idiot!

Tameka

The Puddle of Love

A new guy, Alex, just moved to our school — he's funny, he's cute, and he plays the flute, just like me! He was seated next to me in band, which meant that every Monday and Wednesday, I was guaranteed at least ten or fifteen minutes of small talk with him. Soon, we were really getting to be friends. One day, we were playing a really long song, which meant that a lot of saliva was collecting in my flute. When the song was over, I turned to say something to Alex, and I accidentally dumped out the saliva in my flute — right in Alex's lap! I think I was even more grossed out than he was! I was so embarrassed that in the next class I asked our band teacher to change my seat. Now every time I look at Alex, all I can think of is that wet spot on his jeans.

Michelle

YOU LOOKIN' AT ME?

Sometimes, you don't have to *do* anything embarrassing — people can just look at you and laugh. No, not because you're funny-looking, but because there's something on your shirt or something on your face, because your hair is sticking straight up or there's a big booger hanging out of your nose. If it happens, don't be bummed — at least you can get a good laugh by looking in the mirror!

Forget About It

One day after lunch, I stopped in the bathroom before going back to class. I had to hurry, because I didn't want to be late. When I ran into the classroom, everyone else was already sitting down. They all looked at me and started laughing, but I couldn't figure out why. I sat down in my seat, and the cutie who sits next to me pointed down at my lap. I looked down and saw that I'd forgotten to zip up my jeans. My face turned totally red, and I slouched down in my seat. I've never been so desperate for the school day to end!

Dana

I See London, I See France . . .

I bought a cute new skirt one weekend, so even though it was a little short, I decided to wear it to school on Monday. Before lunch, my teacher asked me to erase the blackboard. I had to stand on a chair to reach the top, but I finally managed to erase everything. I was concentrating so hard that I didn't notice all the people standing around me at first. When I finally looked down, I realized that some of the boys in my class were standing under me, looking right up my skirt!

Nicole

HOW TO HANDLE A HAIR EMERGENCY

Disastrous dye job? Atrocious cut? No need to hide your head until it grows out — check out these top ten ways to deal with a hair crisis.

1. Pull it back in a ponytail. That way, no one can tell what your hair looks like.

2. Tell everyone that this is the latest style from Paris, and they're just behind the trend.

3. Try to convince all your friends to mess up their hair, too, so you can all look bad together.

4. Wear a really wild outfit that will distract people's attention away from the mess on top of your head.

5. Smile and pretend you don't notice what your hair is doing.

6. Call your friends for immediate consultation — someone's bound to have an idea.

7. Check in with a hairdresser about getting a new cut. You never know, maybe he/she can undo the damage.

8. Think everyone will laugh at your hair? Beat them to the punch and be the first to say something funny about it.

9. Remind yourself that your hair isn't nearly as important as what's underneath.

10. When all else fails, wear a hat.

A Sticky Situation

Every year, my school has a carnival, and there's always a bubble-blowing contest. I'm a champion bubble blower, so that's always my favorite part. Last year, I dragged my friends over to the bubble-blowing booth as soon as we got there. I stuffed five pieces of gum in my mouth. Then I blew the biggest bubble of my life! I was so proud of myself — until it popped all over my face and my hair. My mom had to take me home right away to try to get the gum out. I have — or should I say, had — very long, curly hair. There was no way that gum was coming out unless she cut it out. So not only did I miss the carnival, I had to show up at school the next day with a hideously ugly haircut. It took a year for that to grow out — just in time for the next school carnival. Guess which booth I made sure to stay *far* away from that year?

Joanna

Stage Fright

I know this always happens on TV, but I never thought it could actually happen in real life — until it happened to me. Our school was putting on a show, and I had one of the starring roles. At one point in my big solo, I was supposed to lean over and pick something up. When I did, I heard something tear. My costume was a little tight, so I figured that I had just ripped one of the seams. I finished the solo and then turned around to walk off the stage. As I did, the entire auditorium burst into laughter. When I got backstage, someone told me why — the sound I'd heard was my pants ripping! The audience had seen everything! I didn't have another costume, so I had to just pin the pants together with safety pins and hope for the best. I tried to forget it had happened, but the audience didn't. Every time I was onstage, they couldn't stop laughing!

Farah

All Red in the Face

Last fall, there were a couple of really warm days, and one weekend it was even hot enough to go to the beach. I put on a ton of suntan lotion, because I'm always pretty careful about that sort of thing, then went for a swim. When I got out, I figured I should wait until I dried off to put on more lotion. So I just lay out in the sun for a few minutes and shut my eyes. I must have fallen asleep, because I woke up a couple of hours later red as a lobster. The worst part of it all wasn't the pain or the humiliation of having to go to school the next day looking bright red. The worst part was that I'd draped a T-shirt over the top of my face to shield my eyes from the sun. Since that part didn't get sunburned, I had a big white stripe across my bright red face. This lasted for a few endless days — and then my whole face started peeling!

May

Fashion Fiasco

I hate getting up in the morning — I always want those extra few minutes of sleep. One morning, I was running really late, so I was in more of a hurry than usual. I barely had time to brush my hair, then I threw on my jacket and walked to school. There was no time to go to my locker, so I just ran straight to my classroom. I was about to take off my jacket, when I realized I'd forgotten to put on my shirt! I had to spend the entire day wearing my jacket, which wasn't an easy thing to explain.

Mara

Naptime

I fell asleep in class one day, resting my face in my arms. I sit in the back, so no one noticed, and I only woke up when we had to go to our next class. As we walked across the hall, everyone was looking at me really weirdly, and I couldn't figure out why. Then, when we got into the classroom, the teacher gave me a strange look, pulled me aside, and asked, "Arielle, do you need to go to the nurse?" "Why?" I asked. He paused. "Well . . . you seem to have some sort of . . . problem with your face." I ran to the back of the classroom and looked in the mirror — I had been lying on my arm for so long that I had a huge red mark covering the side of my face. What's worse, I didn't want to tell the teacher I had been asleep in class, so I had to go to the nurse and pretend that I didn't know what was wrong with me!

Arielle

Just Clowning Around

My friend and I are always giving each other makeovers. One day, when we were really bored, we decided to do something drastic — we would dye our hair. So we bought some cheap hair dye from the drugstore, followed all the instructions, and waited to see how beautiful we would look. Well, when the dye had set in, my friend looked beautiful — but I looked like a clown! I had always wanted to be a redhead, but my hair wasn't red or auburn — it was a horrible neon orange. I must have washed my hair a thousand times that night, but it didn't help. The next day at school, I still looked like a clown — and I wasn't the only one who thought so. Until it faded out, everyone called me "Bozo"!

Beth

TOTAL GROSS-OUT

Sometimes, something embarrassing happens that's so disgusting, you even gross yourself out. You can only imagine how the people around you must feel! Don't worry — everyone has their own gross-out memories. That means they're probably too busy worrying about their own to remember what happened to you!

That Stinks!

On my way to school, I always pass a house where a really cute puppy lives. I've always wanted a dog and I'm not allowed to have one, but the owner lets me play with him sometimes. As I was passing by one day, the puppy was out on a walk, so I leaned down to scratch his head and say hello. That's when he peed on my leg! I couldn't believe it, and I didn't know what to do. I knew I'd get in trouble if I was late to school, so I had to just keep going. But it was so gross — my foot was squishing in my shoe! When I got there, I hoped no one would notice, but there was no chance of that! As soon as I sat down at my desk, the boy next to me held his nose and said "Ew, what's that smell? Hey, Behnahz peed in her pants!" The teacher eventually sent me home to change my clothes — so I'm sure some people thought that I really did pee in my pants. It was a long time before I went back to visit that puppy again!

Behnahz

HOW TO SURVIVE THE MOST EMBARRASSING DAY OF YOUR LIFE

You just dropped your tray in front of the whole school. Or your pants ripped open and everyone saw your underwear. Or you accidentally dyed your hair bright green.

Hey, stuff happens.

It doesn't have to be the worst day of your life. Here's how you can turn your most embarrassing moment into your most triumphant. People will remember the dumb thing you did, but they'll also remember how you handled it — and they'll be totally impressed.

Step-by-Step Survival Guide

Step 1. *Don't panic.* When something embarrassing happens, your first instinct will probably be to run and hide. But if you stick things out, you might be able to improve the situation.

Step 2. *Remember the three C's: calm, cool, and collected.* That should be you, no matter what happens. Sure, you're blushing on the inside, but you don't need to show it on the outside. If possible (i.e., if it would be at all believable), bluff. "I meant to do that" occasionally works. No matter what, you'll score huge points for keeping your cool.

Step 3. *"I don't care what they think."* Make this your mantra. Repeat it to yourself over and over again, until you actually believe it. Which you should — what do you care what other people think of you? And by the way, no one's going to think less of you because something embarrassing happened (if they do, that's their problem, not yours).

Step 4. *Laugh it off.* Seinfeld knows the secret. So do Jim Carrey and Mike Myers. And here it is — they can't laugh *at* you if they're laughing *with* you. Yes, it's hard to laugh at yourself. But don't take yourself so seriously — better to laugh along with the crowd (or even tell the first joke) than to burst into tears at the first giggle. Don't take this to extremes: There's no need to become the class clown or start making jokes all the time at your own expense. But if everyone's going to be laughing anyway, there's no reason you can't try to control what they're laughing at. Who knows — you may actually decide it was funny!

Step 5. *Get over it.* Sorry to say, but steps 1–4 won't always work. Sometimes, no matter what you do, you're just going to be totally embarrassed. You may think that you'll never be able to live it down. You may never want to leave your house again. In cases like these, there's just one thing left to do: Get over it. Everyone else will. Even if it doesn't seem like it at the time, people forget. They have more important things to worry about than your embarrassing moment — they're probably too busy worrying about their own!

There's No Business Like Show Business

When I'm nervous, I get nosebleeds. There's nothing I can do about it — but fortunately, it doesn't usually happen in public. This one time, however, it did. I was onstage for the dress rehearsal of the school play, I was really nervous, and of course, my nose started bleeding. I didn't even notice it at first, until the blood dripped all the way down my face. Who knows how long it was bleeding?! I didn't know what to do — I mean, the show must go on, but this was ridiculous. Then, just as I was about to run offstage and get a tissue, someone in the props department shouted, "You only get nosebleeds from picking your nose too much." Everyone laughed, and I ran offstage crying.

Leticia

Unprepared

I was taking a math test and I had a runny nose but no tissues. We weren't allowed to get up until we finished the test, and I was too embarrassed to ask the teacher for an exception. So I just tried wiping my nose with my hand and my shirt. But my nose just kept running, and snot was all over my hands. Finally, the teacher came over and really loudly asked if I needed a tissue. The whole class turned to look at me, snot-covered and red-faced. I was so embarrassed. And since I couldn't concentrate on the rest of the test, I totally bombed it!

Sharon

Look Before You Sit

I was sitting on a bench at the bus stop, and it was raining, so I couldn't wait for the school bus to come. Finally, it did, and I hopped on. I usually sit in the back, which means I have to walk past everyone else to get to my seat. As I passed each person, they burst out laughing. At first, I didn't even realize they were laughing at me, until they started shouting things at me. Things like "Hey, she wet her pants!" I didn't know what they were talking about, until my friend leaned over and whispered, "You have a big wet spot on your butt." I must have sat in a puddle at the bus stop — it was the longest bus ride of my life!

Maria

Time to Take the Trash Out

I always take my retainer out during lunch and put it down on my tray. One day, I accidentally threw my retainer away as I was clearing off my lunch tray. The retainer cost so much money that there was no way I could just tell my mom I'd lost it. She'd kill me! So I *had* to find it. The cafeteria workers lent me some rubber gloves so I could dig through the trash. Then I had to suck it up and do it — in front of everyone in the cafeteria. It was gross *and* humiliating.

Nina

Top Secret

One day at school, I was feeling really sick. We were having a party at the end of the day, so I didn't want to go home early. Just after lunch, I got a hall pass to return a book to the library. On the way there, I felt so nauseous that I had to lean against the wall for a second, and then I couldn't help it. I just threw up. The halls were empty so no one saw me. I admit it: I just walked away from the mess I'd made. And I didn't say anything once the rumors started flying about how someone had thrown up in the hallway. No one ever knew it was me, so I guess there's no reason for me to be embarrassed — but I'm still totally humiliated just thinking about it.

Katrinka

Got Snot?

One afternoon after school, I had a sneezing fit in the parking lot. I sneezed all over my hands, but I didn't have any tissues. Since no one was around, I just wiped my hands on my shirt and jeans. I figured no one would know. Wrong. I heard a voice behind me say, "Alison, do you need a tissue?" It was my science teacher. He'd seen the whole thing — and now clearly thought I was a disgusting snot-covered slob!

Alison

School Drool

After my last dentist appointment, I went straight to school, and my mouth was still numb from the Novocain. I didn't realize how numb until I got to lunch. I was drinking my chocolate milk when I suddenly realized that, since I didn't have control over my lips, half of the milk was dribbling down my chin. The next day, someone brought in a baby bottle for me and suggested it might help with my drooling problem.

Keisha

Allergic Reaction

We were working in groups in math class, doing word problems. I was super psyched because I was in a group with Danny, the guy I kind of liked. We were sitting next to each other, leaning our heads in close, trying to figure out this problem. Then suddenly, before I could stop myself, I sneezed, and the snot went flying — all over Danny. He jumped up and shouted, "Gross!" Then he ran out of the classroom to wash himself off. When he came back, he asked to be in a different group. For the rest of the week, he and his friends called me "Snot Rocket." Let's just say that was the end of my crush on Danny.

Janet

Say Cheese

Once, on vacation in California, I saw Brad Pitt, my absolute favorite famous person of all time. He was so nice (and soooo handsome), and he agreed to have his picture taken with me. He actually said, "How could I resist taking a picture with such a beautiful girl?" I thought I was going to faint! After the vacation, I couldn't wait to get the film developed — I was going to frame the picture, put it on my wall, and keep it forever. Then I saw the photo. I couldn't believe it. My mouth was completely orange — I had eaten a bag of Cheetos just beforehand, and they were all stuck in my braces. I'm sure Brad was totally grossed out the whole time he was talking to me. I guess he's an even better actor than I thought!

Denise

All Shook Up

I was in the mall food court, and I was carrying a ton of food, along with a bottle of ketchup for our burgers and fries. On my way back to the table, I tripped and fell — I dropped all the food and the bottle broke. There was red all over my clothes, and I assumed that I had cut myself on the broken glass. I hate the sight of blood, so I freaked out and started crying. Everyone rushed over to help me, and I kept crying, "I'm bleeding, I'm bleeding!" But then my friend looked more closely at my red-stained shirt and said, "Isn't that ketchup?" It was — I hadn't cut myself at all. By this time, a whole crowd was gathered around me. My face turned even redder than my shirt.

Jody

THREE STRIKES AND YOU'RE OUT

Whether you're a sports superstar or an athletic disaster, you've probably had your share of trips, falls, bumps, and misses. Out there on the field, everyone's watching and — if it's a team sport — totally depending on you, which makes it doubly embarrassing to mess up. But as the kids in these sports survival stories show, the best way to handle it is to get right back in the game. If you score the winning basket, no one's going to remember that ten minutes ago you tripped over the ball.

Row, Row, Row Your Boat

Even though I'm a horrible athlete and hate the outdoors, my parents decided that this one summer I should go to overnight camp. We did nothing but sports, sports, sports. The absolute worst was the canoeing. We learned to canoe in the swimming pool. The canoeing itself wasn't that hard, but there was one thing I could never do: pull myself out of the water and back into the canoe. So when we set off on our weeklong canoe trip, I crossed my fingers that I'd never have to do it. Of course, what happens five minutes into the trip? I fall out of the canoe, right into the river. And of course, I couldn't pull myself back in. The other people in my canoe had to haul me back into the boat — it took all of them, and they almost tipped the whole boat over! For the rest of the week, when everyone else jumped out of the canoe to go swimming, I had to sit in the boat and wait. It was a long week.

Misa

Heads Up!

I'm a pretty good athlete, but there's one sport that I just can't stand, and can't play: volleyball. When I found out we were going to play it in gym, I was dreading it. But as it turned out, it wasn't so bad. At least, not at first. After a few games, I thought I might finally be getting the hang of it. The ball was coming right at me. I positioned my hands to volley it — but I misjudged, and the ball hit me right in the face! Not only did my team lose the game, but I ended up with a big black-and-blue mark right in the middle of my forehead.

Jenn

Foul Ball

We were playing kickball in gym, which is my favorite sport because I'm such a great kicker. Sometimes, I can even kick hard enough to get a home run. I waited and waited until I was finally up. It was a perfect pitch, so I slammed the ball, expecting it would go out of the park. Instead, it popped up — and hit me right in the face! It knocked me over, and everyone started laughing at me. It took me a minute, but then I started laughing, too — I must have looked hilarious!

Hannah

Grand Slam

I'm not great at softball — I swing at every pitch and I miss pretty much every ball. The last time I was playing, my gym teacher pitched the ball to me and — I couldn't believe it — the bat actually connected with the ball! Unfortunately, the ball then connected with my gym teacher's head. The whole gym class started laughing. I did, too, which was my big mistake — I'm convinced my gym teacher still hates me.

Nisha

HOW TO ACT WHEN YOU'RE NOT THE ONE

Sometimes, you get lucky. Sometimes, you're not the one embarrassing yourself; you're the one watching. You're probably tempted to laugh (after all, when it's not you, these things are usually pretty funny). But remember the Golden Rule: Treat others as you'd want them to treat you.

Be sympathetic, not sarcastic. The person will be grateful that at least one person isn't laughing at him/her. And later on, when you're the one in the hot seat, maybe you'll have at least one friendly face in the crowd!

Of course, sometimes, you just can't help yourself. If you *do* laugh, don't hate yourself for it — funny is funny. Just remember to be nice about it — even if you laugh when someone falls, you can still offer a hand to help him/her up.

A Downhill Climb

This year, I went skiing for the first time, and at first I was doing pretty well. So well that my friends convinced me to leave the bunny slope and try out a harder one. It went fine — until I fell down. I didn't get hurt — but I couldn't get up again. Every time I tried to stand on one foot, my ski would just start sliding down the mountain and I'd fall over. Even my friends couldn't haul me up. After a few minutes, the ski patrol sped up to make sure everything was all right. After they heard what happened, they helped me up. They told me that if I couldn't get up after a fall, I'd better go back to the bunny slope! I was so embarrassed that I hiked down the mountain with my skis off. I spent the rest of the day in the ski lodge, drinking hot chocolate and feeling sorry for myself.

Anh

Soccer Star

I'm terrible at soccer — whenever I try to kick the ball, I usually miss it. I have no eye-foot co-ordination. So usually, when I play, I try to stay far away from the ball. It works for me. But this year in gym, we have a teacher who's really into everyone taking part in the game, and I knew she'd never go for that. So when we finally played soccer in gym, I actually started running after the ball. And you know what? I wasn't as bad as I thought. I actually passed the ball a couple of times, and once I managed to dribble it partway across the field. But my best move came at the end, when I saw an opening and took it — I slammed the ball with my foot and sent it flying into the goal! I started cheering, but no one else did. In fact, my team was frowning, and the other team was just laughing. I didn't get it, until my friend explained: I'd just scored the winning goal for the wrong team!

Jessica

Next Stop, the Olympics!

Last Christmas vacation, I went ice-skating with some friends at our local skating rink. When we got there, we noticed that a couple of hotties from school were already there, and we did everything we could to impress them. I used to take skating lessons when I was little, so I thought I would get their attention by practicing some spins and jumps in the middle of the rink. I was looking pretty good until I tried a particularly hard jump, tripped over my skates, and fell flat on my face. I got their attention all right. I also got a broken nose!

Blair

Get Shorty

I'm really short, but that's okay, I'm used to it. Except occasionally, when it causes me *big* problems, like last month in gym class. We were doing gymnastics, and we were learning how to vault over the pommel horse. That meant we had to run down a narrow strip of carpet, jump on a springboard, and push ourselves up and over the horse. No problem, right? Well, it was no problem for everyone else. But when I ran down and jumped on the springboard, I barely got high enough to *see* over the horse, much less get over it. So I just slammed right into it. The whole class started laughing — and so did my gym teacher.

Christina

Just One of the Guys

I'm a total tomboy — I'd way rather be playing soccer or softball than going to the mall and spending a boring day shopping. But a lot of times, guys don't want a girl on their team, so I always feel like I have to prove myself. Last week, I was in the park, and a bunch of guys from school were playing touch football. I talked them into letting me play, but they didn't seem too happy about it. So I played extra hard, just to prove that I could do it. I was going out for a pass, without looking where I was going — and I ran right into a tree. I slammed into it and fell backward onto the ground. They all thought it was the funniest thing they'd ever seen. But they were totally impressed when I got right up and started playing again!

Sherry

Go, Team, Go!

When Sean, the boy I liked, asked me to go to a basketball game with him, I was totally psyched — even though I don't know anything about basketball. A few minutes into the game, everyone around us jumped to their feet and started cheering. When I asked Sean what had happened, he looked at me like I was crazy. "We just scored," he said. After that, I tried to pay closer attention to the game. When the next player scored, I was the first one out of my seat, yelling and screaming. Then I looked around. I was the only one on our side of the arena who was standing up. Everyone else was sitting there and looking at me. Now Sean looked at me like I was *really* crazy. "I thought we scored," I said. He shook his head. "No, we didn't score — you're cheering for the wrong team." Oops.

Maggie

A for Effort

I'm usually horrible in gym class, which is why I was so proud of myself when I got an A in gymnastics. Our gym teacher, who we all disliked, was out for the month, so the substitute graded us instead. She was just as hard on us as our normal gym teacher, but she was at least a little nicer. Well, when our gym teacher finally returned, she wasn't in a great mood to begin with. Then she watched us go through our gymnastics, and that didn't help. She thought we were terrible! She made us all sit down as she looked over the grade book. Then she started yelling about how the substitute had been too easy on us and gave us all better grades than we deserved. And then, in front of everyone, she said, "There are people here, like Janice, who couldn't possibly have deserved an A. I'm sure she can't even do a somersault." Everyone turned to look at me and my face turned bright red. How could she say something like that?

Janice

FAMILY MATTERS

You love your family.

You really do.

At least, most of the time.

Well-meaning parents, pesky little brothers, and obnoxious older sisters, not to mention all your aunts, uncles, and cousins — sometimes it seems like there are hundreds of relatives out there, just waiting to embarrass you. Of course they don't mean to do it; they love you. But sometimes, you may wish you had just been hatched from an egg!

All in the Family

My mom is *really* into togetherness. She thinks that our family will only work if we spend "quality time" together, every week. One weekend, we were supposed to go to an amusement park. I was psyched, because usually we go to some boring museum. But then my mother brought out the shirts. Hideous, bright-colored, flowered shirts — one for each of us. She wanted us all to dress alike, and she wanted us all to dress like that! She even had matching hats. She thought this would help our "togetherness" — and keep us from getting lost. What could I do? I figured that at least no one would see me. Wrong. As soon as we got to the ticket line, I spotted my friend Jessica and some other kids from school. I slouched down, hoping they wouldn't see me. But my mom saw them. "Isn't that your little friend from school?" she asked. Then she waved over at the group of them and pointed at me. "Yoo-hoo, Jessica, over here — look who's here, too!" Jessica and all her friends looked up, spotted me, and came right over. No way were they going to miss the chance to laugh at me in my family outfit — and they didn't miss the chance to tell *everyone* at school about it the next day!

Marisa

The Happiest Place on Earth?

Every summer, my family goes on a big family vacation. This year was Disney World and Epcot. On our last night in Epcot, we went to eat at the American Pavilion (I'm a picky eater, and that's the only type of food I would eat). Halfway through dinner, I laughed so hard that I choked on my hot dog. I couldn't breathe! Our cute waiter came over to try to help, just as I finally coughed up the chunk of hot dog — right in his face. I can't blame this embarrassing moment on my family — it was all me!

Janelle

Here Comes the . . . Oops!

I was so honored when my favorite aunt asked me to be a bridesmaid at her wedding. The day of the wedding, for the first time in my life, I felt really beautiful — I had a gorgeous bridesmaid's dress, a fancy hairdo, and even had fresh flowers wound through my hair. As I was walking down the aisle, I felt like a graceful princess. At least until I tripped over my dress and fell flat on the floor. My bouquet went flying everywhere, and all the other bridesmaids rushed over to help me up. Let's just say it spoiled the mood.

Lauren

HOW TO DEAL WITH YOUR EMBARRASSING FAMILY

Families: You can't live with 'em, and you're not old enough to live by yourself! So what do you do? You know your parents love you, so why can't they stop themselves from totally humiliating you in front of your friends? And your twerpy little sib — just because you *accidentally* broke his toy, is that any reason for him to take your diary to school? Is he *trying* to ruin your life? Face it: Sometimes your family is going to embarrass you. What can you say to everyone else when they do? Here are a few suggestions:

"These people? I've never seen them before in my life!"

"You think my little sister is so cute? Then why don't you take her home with you."

"Sorry about my little brother — he was raised by wild beasts."

***DON'T FORGET: These are all just jokes. You love your family. You really do. No matter how much they may totally, completely, absolutely embarrass you. . . .

Zack Attack

I keep a diary, and I write in it every night. I write down everything that happens in my life — what makes me happy and what makes me sad, who my friends are, and who I think is cute. Not to mention all my deepest, darkest secrets. So you can imagine how upset I was when it suddenly disappeared. I knew my little brother, Zack, had hidden it somewhere, but I couldn't figure out where, and I couldn't get him to admit anything. I tried to forget about it — I figured that eventually he'd get bored with his stupid game and give it back to me. Well, a couple of days later in school, one of the cutest guys in our class came up to me. I was so excited — this was the first time he'd ever talked to me! He looked kind of awkward, and I thought, *Maybe this is it, maybe he's actually going to ask me out.* But instead, he reached into his backpack and pulled out . . . my diary. "Um, my little brother got this from your little brother," he said. "I thought you might want it back." I ripped it out of his hands and stuffed it into my bag — I still don't know whether he read it or not! Why, why do I have to have a little brother?

Natalie

Mall Misery

This Christmas, my Aunt Martha knitted me a bright pink wool sweater with a big reindeer on it. I thought it was the most hideous thing I'd ever seen. My plan was to stick it in a drawer and never look at it again. Or maybe even throw it out. But my mom had other ideas. Not only did she make me keep the sweater but she made me *wear* it. In public! I wore it to the mall, and since it was the day after Christmas, everyone was there. Who did I run into first? The boy I had a huge crush on and all of his friends. Now he probably thinks this is how I like to dress!

Abbie

Cleanup, Aisle 7!

I was in the grocery store with my mom and my sister, and I *really* needed to go. There's no bathroom in our grocery store, and my mom was taking forever. Finally, I couldn't hold it anymore, and (I can hardly bear to say it) I wet my pants. I didn't know what to do — there was a big wet spot and I was sure everyone could see. I was hoping I could make it out of the store and into the car without anyone noticing, but of course, my little sister notices everything. "Mom, Mom, Stephanie went bathroom!" she announced loudly. Everyone in the checkout line turned to look at me. I think my mother was (almost) as embarrassed as I was!

Stephanie

My Birthday Suit

Last year on my birthday, my parents told me they were taking me to a show. They were due home at seven, and we would have to leave right after that. So when I realized it was six-thirty, and I hadn't even started getting dressed, I freaked out. I took a quick shower and then realized that the shirt I wanted to wear was still in the laundry room. Since no one was home, I just ran downstairs in my underwear. But when I got to the bottom of the stairs of my supposedly empty house, a crowd of people was standing at the bottom, waiting for me. They cheered and shouted, "Happy Birthday!" It was a surprise party. Well, I was surprised all right — I stood there in shock for a moment and then raced upstairs in tears. Even though it was my party, I refused to come down for the rest of the night.

Taylor

Slip 'n' Slide

My family was on vacation in Jamaica, and we actually got the chance to climb a waterfall! There was a group of about fifty people. We all linked hands and then hiked up the side of the waterfall — that way, the person above you could help you over really rocky parts. It was fun, and so beautiful, but it was also really slippery — you had to be very careful not to fall. And of course, I did! My foot skidded over a wet rock, and I didn't just fall down, I slid about ten feet down the waterfall! But the worst part was that, since we were all holding hands, I dragged down the person above me and several of the people below me. It was like a people avalanche, and it was all my fault! I came back to the hotel that day wet, bruised, and totally humiliated.

Campbell

A Series of Unfortunate Events

My younger brother has an embarrassing problem — he wets his pants. A lot. When he does it in school, the nurse usually calls my mom to come and bring him new pants and underwear. Well, one day, I was sitting in class and I saw the nurse knock on the door of my classroom. My teacher went over to talk to her, and the nurse handed him something. Then the nurse left, and my teacher came over to my desk, cleared his throat, and said, "Your mother dropped this off for you." He handed me a clear plastic bag — containing pants and a pair of underwear! The nurse had brought it to the wrong classroom! I explained it to everyone who was sitting around me, but who knows whether they believed me. I know it wasn't my brother's fault, but I still haven't forgiven him for that one!

Corinne

Hair Horror

At the beginning of every summer, my mother always used to take me to get a haircut. My mother believes that long hair is too hot for the summer. She made me get it cut short — and not cute short. Ugly short. I always thought it made me look like a boy, but my mother told me I was being ridiculous. So every May, I walked into the haircutting place looking like a normal girl and walked out looking totally lame. Well, one year, we went shopping right after I got a haircut, even though all I wanted to do was go home and cry. My mother ran into someone she worked with and stopped to talk to her for a minute. The woman looked down at me and said to my mother, "Oh, I didn't realize that you had a son, too. What a handsome young boy." I burst into tears and ran to the car. I don't think my mother was any happier than I was — that was the last year I had to get my summer cut.

Chantal

Mommy Dearest

My mom gets home from work after I get home from school, so she usually leaves a message for me with some afternoon chores. One day, I came home from school with my new friend Samantha. Before we went downstairs to watch TV, we listened to the message on the machine. It was my mom. "Hi, sweetie, I just wanted to remind you to take out the trash. Also, since you were so upset by it last night, I've decided that you don't have to throw out Mr. Snuffles after all. He may be all worn out, but he is *your* bunny, and since it means that much to you, why don't you keep him? But don't think that this means having a temper tantrum like that will ever work again! Love you, honey!" The message ended. I couldn't say anything, and I couldn't look at Samantha. I couldn't believe she'd just heard that. Not only did she now know about Mr. Snuffles, but she knew I'd had a temper tantrum last night when Mom wanted to throw him out! She didn't say anything, but she must have thought I was such a loser! Now I always send my friends downstairs *before* I listen to the messages from Mom.

Jacqui

WHAT ARE FRIENDS FOR?

There's nothing funnier than seeing one of your friends do something stupid — unless you're the one who does it, and your friends are the ones getting all the big laughs. You and your friends usually go through everything together, but when it comes to being embarrassed, you feel totally on your own! Don't forget — they may be laughing, but they don't mean anything by it. And the next day, they'll probably be the ones doing something embarrassing. And then you'll be totally understanding and not laugh at all. Right?

Doggy Disaster

I was so excited when my new friend Michelle invited me over to her house for the first time. And what a house! Unlike my house, where you can't walk in the door without tripping over something, hers was so empty and clean that it looked like no one lived there. All the furniture was white, and so was the rug, so I was extra careful not to spill anything on it. A little while after I got there, her mother came into the room to check on us. She wrinkled up her nose and asked us what that horrible smell was. I hadn't wanted to say anything, because I thought it would be rude. But she was right: Something stunk. Well, it only took a second for Michelle's mom to discover the culprit: me! She pointed down at my shoe. Michelle's dog had made a mess on the lawn, and I guess I stepped in it on the way in the house. Not only did it smell horrible but I'd tracked it into her house — all over her white rug. I don't think I'll be invited back there anytime soon!

Yvonne

Candid Camera

I had a doctor's appointment, and I was meeting some friends afterward. As I was taking the elevator down to meet them in the lobby, I started picking my nose — I didn't have any tissues with me, and I figured there was no one to see me do it. When the elevator hit the lobby, I quickly stopped. The doors opened, and my friends were all waiting outside the elevators. They were staring at something right above the elevator doors, and when they saw me, they burst into laughter. I didn't understand why until I saw what they were staring at. The elevator must have had a camera in it, because there was a little TV screen above the elevator doors that showed everything that was going on inside — including me, picking my nose. The first place we went that afternoon was the bathroom, so I could wash my hands!

Carla

Don't Make Me Laugh

My friends are always making fun of me for how easy it is to make me laugh. And it's true — I always laugh really hard, even at the lamest jokes. I just can't help myself! At lunch, they like to compete with one another to see who can make me laugh the most. One day, the guy I was crushing on came to have lunch with us. My friends were even funnier than usual, and finally, my BFF said something that I thought was hysterical. Even though no one else was laughing, I couldn't stop myself. I laughed so hard that the milk I was drinking shot out of my nose — and spattered on the hottie across the table. After that, I was the only person at the table *not* laughing. I guess there's a first time for everything!

Eve

Fast-Forward

One Saturday, I sent my friend an e-mail listing all the boys in our class, grading them on smartness, niceness, and cuteness. The ones who got an A+ on cuteness had little smiley faces and heart icons around their names. The next Monday in school, I noticed that people were looking at me a little strangely and kept whispering as I walked by. I didn't get it. Then I met up with my older sister after school, and she told me why. Apparently, my friend thought the list was so funny that she forwarded it to all her friends. And they forwarded it to *their* friends, and so on, until even the people in my sister's class got it. And of course, *all* the boys saw it, too. I've never been so humiliated — and I'm still not speaking to my so-called friend!

Isabelle

Supermarket Stumble

I was in the grocery store with my friends, picking up junk food for our weekly movie night. The cookies that we wanted were blocked by a tall display of cans, so I squeezed in around it to get what we needed. I guess I didn't squeeze carefully enough. My arm brushed the tower of cans and knocked them all over — I'm sure the entire store heard the loud crash. Then the store manager came over and kicked us out! The next weekend we decided to get our junk food at the local convenience store instead.

Naomi

Wild Kingdom

My friends and I started a pet-sitting business to make some extra money, and we decided we needed to drum up some publicity. We agreed that the next day, we would each dress as a different animal. I was supposed to be a bunny. I knew my mother would never go for it, but fortunately, she leaves for work before I leave for school, so I could put on my costume without her knowing. I got to school and looked for my BFFs — I couldn't wait to see them in their animal outfits. Well, there they were, all right — all wearing their normal clothes. Their mothers had forbidden them to wear anything so foolish to school. Which left me looking like a big fool, all by myself!

Zoe

FIRST IMPRESSIONS (AND HOW TO MAKE PEOPLE FORGET THEM)

Maybe you've heard the expression "You never get a second chance to make a first impression." That may be true but only technically. If you make a first impression that happens to be, well, totally humiliating, don't freak out. Sure, it's great if you can make a fabulous first impression. But sometimes you're just not that lucky.

So what if you make a fool out of yourself the first time you meet someone? It's not the end of the world. It's certainly no reason to give up. While you'll never get to make another first impression, you can make a second one whenever you want (even a third and fourth one, if necessary).

And you can make sure that *second* impression is a good one. Here's something else to keep in mind: If you really embarrassed yourself in front of someone, chances are, they'll remember you. The first problem in getting to know someone is making yourself stick in their mind — and you've already got that one all taken care of!

In Over My Head

I was going to a pool party, but I didn't know how to swim. I didn't want to look like a loser, so I figured I would just learn as I went along. I figured, How hard could it be? Pretty hard, as it turns out. I was doing fine in the shallow end, but then everyone started jumping into the deep end. That looked like fun, so I did it, too. The jumping part was fine — but once I was in the water, I didn't know what to do. It was too deep to stand, so I started flailing around and screaming. I was afraid I was going to drown! My friend's father had to jump in the pool with all his clothes on and rescue me. I was fine, but they sent me home, which is probably a good thing, since I couldn't face anyone at the party! The next day, I begged my mother to sign me up for swimming lessons.

Maddy

How Could He?

Abbie and Melissa, the coolest girls in my class, barely spoke to me before last month. Then for some reason, they seemed to decide that I was cool enough to be their friend. A couple of weeks later, I invited them over for a sleepover, and I couldn't believe it when they said yes! It was going along great — we were in the basement, watching a movie and eating popcorn. They actually seemed to think that I was cool, too. Then the phone rang, and I went to answer it — big mistake. When I came back downstairs, my twerpy little brother was there, holding an armful of humiliating stuff from my bedroom: my old blankie, the stuffed rabbit I still sleep with, and some old Power Rangers sheets. Abbie and Melissa were cracking up. That's the last time I invite anyone over to my house while *he's* around!

Bridget

Dude, Where's My Dog?

My friends and I wanted to make some extra money, so we started a dog-walking service. Since I'm the tallest, they always stuck me with the biggest dogs. One day, I was walking Heidi, a big, beautiful golden retriever. Stronger than I expected — halfway down the street, she pulled the leash out of my hands (though not before she pulled me down on the ground and dragged me halfway down the block!) and ran away. I chased after her, but it was no use. The dog disappeared. I walked around the neighborhood for hours, but I couldn't find the dog anywhere. Finally, hot, tired, and totally humiliated, I knocked on my neighbor's door to tell her that I had lost her dog. As soon as she opened the door, I heard a bark, and Heidi came bounding up behind her owner's legs. The dog had come back right after I lost it. If only I hadn't been too embarrassed to admit I'd lost the dog, I could have saved myself a long and terrible afternoon.

Debbie

I Dare You

I don't play truth or dare anymore, and here's why: The last time I played, someone dared me to go upstairs, dress up in sheets and pillowcases (*only* sheets and pillowcases), and then dance down the stairs. Well, it took me a while to put together my outfit, but I finally got it perfectly arranged. I danced down the stairs with a sheet wrapped around my body and a pillowcase on my head — and only then did I notice that my girlfriends weren't the only ones in the room. While I was upstairs, my friend's older brother and all of his friends had come home, and everyone was hanging out in the living room. The boys all looked up at me and started laughing and whistling. I can't believe no one warned me they were there!

Aminche

Wet and Wild

I like dogs, but I admit, I get a little scared when they're really big and *really* enthusiastic. At the last pool party I went to, the birthday girl had an enormous white, shaggy dog. I don't know why, but he started chasing me around. They say that if a dog is chasing you, you shouldn't run, because then it thinks you want to play. I know that now, but unfortunately, I didn't know it then. The dog was chasing me, so I ran. And it ran after me. We ran around in circles all over the deck until finally the dog took a flying leap at me and I stumbled backward, right into the pool! Well, that stopped the dog — but now I had a new problem: I was in the pool with all my clothes on. I was drenched, and everyone was laughing. For the rest of the party, every few minutes someone would shout, "Look out behind you, it's the dog!"

Kathleen

MOVING ON

Now tell the truth. Has anything this embarrassing ever happened to you? Hopefully, you're lucky, and you've made it this far in life without suffering through this kind of complete and utter humiliation. But even if you have had a totally miserable moment, now at least you know that you're not alone.

Everyone in this book suffered through the embarrassment of spilling things, dropping things, losing their clothing, their balance, or their lunch. And they're not the only ones. Whether it involves food, falls, sports, or snot, if you can imagine it, chances are, it's happened to someone. Possibly even someone you know . . .

No matter who it is, no matter what happened to them, they all have one thing in common: They all survived.

And believe it or not, so will you!